Translated by Emma Lunt

A Journey to the Centre of the Earth

BY JULES VERNE

BrightSummaries.com

BOOK ANALYSIS

BOOK ANALYSIS
Bright
Summaries.com
Fifty Shades
of Grey Trilogy

JULES VERNE

FRENCH NOVELIST

- **Born in Nantes in 1828**
- **Died in Amiens in 1905**
- **Notable works:**
    - *A Journey to the Centre of the Earth* (1864), novel
    - *Around the World in Eighty Days* (1873), novel
    - *The Mysterious Island* (1874), novel

Jules Verne, who was born in Nantes in 1828, firstly began studying law and then, from 1852 onwards, published a play and several short stories. He also became friends with the adventurer Jacques Arago (French author and explorer) and met explorers and scientists. His first novel, *Five Weeks in a Balloon* (1863) was greatly successful. It was the start of the *Voyages extraordinaries* ('extraordinary journeys') collection that consisted of 18 short stories and 65 novels including *A Journey to the Centre of the Earth* (1864), *Twenty Thousand Leagues Under the Sea* (1869), *Around the World in Eighty Days* (1873), *The Mysterious Island* (1874) and *Michael Strogoff: The Courier of the Czar* (1876), among other. These well-researched works which mix adventure, science fiction and fantasy, reflect the author's interest in the technological advances of his time and his love for travel.

In 1886, the death of his editor and friend, Jules Hetzel, and his declining interest in science marked a turning point in his career. He died in Amiens in 1905. Today, he is one of the most translated French-language authors in the world.

JOURNEY TO THE CENTRE OF THE EARTH

FROM SCIENCE TO SCIENCE FICTION

- **Genre:** adventure novel
- **Reference edition:** Verne, J. (1872) *A Journey to the Centre of the Earth*. Trans. Unknown. London: Griffith and Farran.
- **First edition:** 1864
- **Themes:** travel, adventure, science fiction, nature, prehistoric, exploration

A Journey to the Centre of the Earth is the third novel from the *Voyages extraordinaires* collection by Jules Verne. It was published for the first time in 1864. The year in which the novel was written actually corresponds to the time of the story, which is set in 1863. The author therefore throws the reader into an era that he knows well.

In his novel, Verne develops the chemistry that combines science with visionary dreams that is characteristic of him. He presents an old, German scholar and geologist, accompanied by his clumsy and cowardly 19-year-old nephew, who is the narrator: they undertake an improbable journey scattered with increasingly surprising adventures.

SUMMARY

CHAPTERS 1-5

Hamburg, 24 May 1863. Professor Hardwigg suddenly returns home to seek refuge in his cupboard from which he insistently calls his nephew Harry. The source of this hurry is the purchase of an Icelandic manuscript from the 12th century written in runes. This event requires the full attention of the uncle, who even loses his appetite for it.

A parchment has been separated from the manuscript. It is in the hands of the chemist Arne Saknussemm and dates back to the 14th century, at the earliest. Harry tries to decode this strange writing and finally cracks the secret code: a dangerous and fascinating journey awaits them, but he decides to destroy the document to avoid this.

The uncle appears but Harry stays silent. The uncle puts everybody on a diet as long as the code is not discovered. Under pressure, Harry reveals the secret.

CHAPTERS 6-10

The message describes a journey to the centre of the Earth, by entering through an Icelandic volcano, Sneffels. Harry shares his worries with his uncle and mother. Harry's girlfriend, Gretchen, finally convinces him to leave with his uncle.

Having arrived in Copenhagen, the professor goes in search

of a boat going to Iceland. While waiting for the departure, he makes his nephew do exercises to overcome vertigo.

Eleven days later, they meet some important people from Reykjavik: Governor Trampe, Mayor Finsen and Professor Fridriksson. The two Germans are invited to Fridriksson's table who tells them the story of Arne Saknussemm and of the extinct volcano. Fridriksson will introduce them to a good guide.

CHAPTER 11-15

The following day, they meet the guide, Hans Bjelke, who will accompany them throughout the journey. On the morning of 16 June, the expedition is launched.

The Icelandic landscape is poor and desolate. They cross the country by horse and sometimes by boat, notably to cross a fjord. Having once again experienced Icelandic hospitality, the travellers reach the first lava flows. On 22 June, they are at the foot of the Sneffels and stay with a local in the small town of Stapi.

The ascension of Sneffels begins, slowly and silently. Hans leads the way and warns of danger. The midnight sun awaits them at the summit.

CHAPTERS 16-20

The adventurers descend into the crater. They discover the inscription "Arne Saknussemm", then descend down the volcano's chimney on a small set of stairs. Ten hours later, they reach the bottom.

They then move towards the depths of the Earth down a small corridor. The heat is bearable, despite how deep they are. Harry, however, is worried. Finally arriving at the tunnel, they are faced with two paths. The uncle chooses to go towards the east, but it seems that the travellers are returning towards the surface.

Water becomes scarce. They cross a coal mine and Harry observes the geological strata, showing the Earth's evolution. A wall eventually obstructs the passage.

CHAPTERS 21-25

They have to turn back. They decide, despite everything, to pursue their mission. Thirsty and tired by the walk, Harry faints, imagining that they are in a granite prison. Upon awakening, Hans, who has heard the sound of a torrent from far away, drills a hole in the rock: out springs boiling and ferruginous water. The stream is baptised "Hansbach" (meaning *Hans Brook*). This event rekindles young Harry's courage. They are now five leagues deep, below the Atlantic.

After arriving at a cave at a depth of sixteen leagues, the travellers rest. The professor and his nephew spend their time thinking about scientific considerations.

CHAPTERS 26-30

Little by little, Hans' silence spreads to them. On 7 August, Harry loses sight of his two companions and the spring that accompanied them on their descent. Harry falls into despair. His lamp gradually dulls. Panicked, he bangs his head and loses consciousness. It is therefore completely dark. He finally awakens and hears a noise in the distance. The wall guides his voice and that of his uncle. They are one league apart. Harry follows the path of the sound and stumbles.

Upon awakening, he is close to his companions and is happy to see them again. He discovers the Hardwigg Ocean, secluded in an enormous cavity. The huge mushrooms and gigantic bones, witnesses of the nature of another time, amaze them.

CHAPTERS 31-35

The exploration of this new world continues in the Hardwigg Ocean. Hans catches a blind fish from another era, which causes Harry to dream about the subject of evolution and prehistoric animals. The lack of earth in sight provokes the professor's impatience. Suddenly, a terrible fight breaks out between two prehistoric marine animals, then calm returns. A monstrous mass then appears in the distance, which is in fact a geyser. The obstacle is overcome and navigation continues.

The weather is stormy and the professor's mood is dark. It is then that a ball of fire threatens them, carries the mast away, then disappears. They finally reach dry land.

CHAPTERS 36-40

Professor Hardwigg realises that the wind has taken them

back up the river that they had left. Hans repairs the damage while the professor and his nephew explore the region. They come across an immense cemetery of prehistoric animals and, suddenly, a human skull, then many entire skeletons. The professor begins theorising that this was an amphitheatre.

They discover colossal trees, frightening mastodons and a giant being that commands them. Turning around, Harry finds a rusty dagger. A little later, they discover two letters engraved in a tunnel: "A.S." like Arne Saknussemm. The investigations continue but the two Germans encounter a rock that obstructs their passage: they must blow it up.

CHAPTERS 41-45

Harry lights the fuse. Following the explosion, an abyss opens that sucks up the sea and carries them away with the raft onto which they had retreated. The fall is dizzying. Then, having arrived in a well, the raft gradually climbs back up. The heat suddenly becomes unbearable and the water is boiling: a volcanic eruption is about to happen. They were actually in the chimney of an active volcano. Harry faints in the heat.

When Harry awakens, the travellers are on the mountainside and half-naked, in a magnificent region. It is Stromboli. They pretend to be shipwrecked sailors.

On 9 September, they return to Hamburg. The professor recounts his journey to incredulous scientists. A book is written about this journey, which earns them recognition throughout the world. Happy and proud of his uncle, Harry marries Gretchen.

CHARACTER STUDY

PROFESSOR VON HARDWIGG

An original character, named wrongly due to an incorrect pronunciation, Professor Hardwigg is the instigator of the journey. He is the head of the family in the house at 19 Köningstrasse, where Martha, the servant, Harry and, occasionally, Gretchen, also live.

A selfish and miserly scholar, as well as a "very learned man" (Chapter 1), he is a geologist, mineralogist, and a university professor. He is also a custodian of a museum and has a large book collection, which explains his enthusiasm for the ancient manuscript. He speaks quite a few languages fluently (German, French, Icelandic, Latin, English, Italian, etc.).

He is rich, tall, thin, blonde and seems young for a man of 50. He wears glasses and has a love for tobacco. His passion for discovery and sciences make him an impetuous, courageous and passionate man, varying between insanity and genius. Despite his grumpy nature, he does not lack humanity and even shows altruism towards his nephew.

HARRY

Harry is the story's narrator. An orphan, he is the adopted nephew of Professor Hardwigg. Harry was born in 1844. He is therefore 19 years old. This young man is in love with Gretchen, a pretty 17-year-old girl from Virland, Professor

Hardwigg's goddaughter.

He is passionate about mineralogy and conscientiously helps his uncle with his work. Less knowledgeable than the professor, his perceptiveness nevertheless allows him to find the key to deciphering Arne Saknussemm's code. Incapable of going without food and his girlfriend, Harry reveals the parchment code to the professor, which leads to the journey to the centre of the Earth.

His fearful and cowardly nature contrasts with Hans's rigour and his uncle's courage. He finds the spectacle that he observes in the depths of the Earth surprisingly fascinating. Thus, we discover the qualities of the young scientist who is passionate about geology and evolution. His adventure companions save his life numerous times. His many blackouts break up the narration of the story, which reinforces the novel's extraordinary nature.

HANS BEJLKE

Hans is a sturdy Icelandic con man, tall and energetic. A true force of nature, he is quiet and serene, just like the Icelandic landscape. He has long, red hair and small blue eyes that portray an intelligent gaze. He also hunts eiders, a type of migrating bird whose feathers are a source of wealth in Iceland.

Mainly speaking Danish, Hans never communicates with Harry. He is generally not very talkative at all and only speaks when it is necessary. Professor Hardwigg takes on the task of translating what he says for his nephew.

He has a spirit of initiative and is a precious help for the two Germans, as he is constantly devoted to his task as a guide. He finds water (Hansbach), when the reserves are dwindling and saves Harry from drowning several times. Every Saturday for the thirteen weeks, the professor pays him the agreed amount.

When Harry finds them back (Chapter 29), Hans shows some joy, which proves that he is not devoid of humanity.

PROFESSOR FRIDRIKSSON

He welcomes the professor and his nephew into his home in Iceland. He is very hospitable and courteous with his guests. A professor of natural sciences, a modest scholar who speaks only Latin and Icelandic, he is one of the few characters with whom Harry can communicate (in Latin).

It is he who reveals to Professor Hardwigg the reputation of Arne Saknussemm, an Icelandic scholar who was persecuted in the 16th century. He also tells them that Sneffels has been extinct for a long time and introduces them to a reliable guide. He is therefore a key character.

ANALYSIS

A PARTICULAR STRUCTURE: JOURNEYS WITHIN THE JOURNEY

The novel's structure is remarkable, as much in terms of the style as the content. *A Journey to the Centre of the Earth* is more than a simple trip to space:

- The chapters are very regular. Each one generally contains a principle action that marks a shift in time (a day or more) and space (towards a new destination). The story plays out over a little more than three months (from 24 May to 9 September 1863), and is set in several countries, on Earth and inside Earth. Most of the chapters end with a night of well-deserved rest for the characters.
- The protagonists are always on the go, in search of a destination which they get closer to but never reach: the centre of the Earth. Having entered the Earth through an extinct volcano in the northwest of Europe (in Iceland), they leave through another volcano, this time an active one, situated in the south of Europe (in Sicily). The structure is therefore cyclic.
- The characters evolve throughout their expedition (maiden voyage) as Harry becomes a man and can marry Gretchen, while the professor can develop his scientific theories and he is greeted as a hero after his journey.
- It talks about a journey in time as well as in space. As the days wear on, the characters sink further into the depths of the Earth, and make the reverse journey of the evolution of the planet and of species. They concretely

discover the different eras of the Earth, as well as the fauna and the flora of these eras (prehistoric animals, fossils, etc.).

- The physical advancement of the characters is vertical and horizontal. The horizontal dimension (for example, the navigation of the Hardwigg Ocean, the Mediterranean's alter ego) puts the professor in a bad mood as it does not bring him any closer to his goal, while the dizzying falls excite him.
- The theme of the journey materialises as an essential object: the compass. During the storm on the Hardwigg Ocean, the polarity of the poles is reversed and makes the travellers literally lose the north. This 'loss of direction' appears to add to the two dimension of space and time that are many themselves, which throws the protagonists into the labyrinthine structure.
- Harry's numerous blackouts create a dreamlike dimension that reinforces the extraordinary aspect of the journey through ellipses and his dreams.
- Harry keeps a logbook during the crossing of the Hardwigg Ocean. The story of the journey to the centre of the Earth is also published at the end of the novel. This mise en abyme gives Jules Verne's novel a supplementary dimension. Mise en abyme is an artistic method that consists of representing a work within a work of the same type (for example, we can look at the theatre within a theatre in *L'Illusion Comique* by Corneille (1635) or Russian dolls).

FROM SCIENCE TO SCIENCE FICTION

Science plays an essential part in this novel. From geology

to palaeontology, passing through mineralogy, chemistry, physics and cryptology, science shows the advancement in the knowledge of the time. Professor Hardwigg notably believes in the theory of Humphry Davy (British scientist, 1778-1829) according to which there is not excessive internal heat at the centre of the Earth.

The units of measurement used throughout the novel reinforce the serious, previse and scientific nature: knots, feet, leagues, etc. It works on a metric, Anglo-Saxon system.

Furthermore, the professor brings a great number of measurement tools on his expedition (see Chapter 11): two compasses, a manometer, a thermometer of Eigel, a chronometer and two devices from Ruhmkorff (German scientist, 1803-1877) which serve as waterproof electric lamps.

By emphasising these scientific advances, the author is credited for an authentic and scientifically accurate story. The scientific theories are a definitive work and cannot be false. What is revealed by science fiction (the journey in the Earth, an underground world, the return through a volcano, etc.) is confirmed as scientific and therefore appears to be believable and credible, while it is purely fictional.

THE ISSUE OF LANGUAGE

The theme of travel encourages the use of quite a few languages in the novel:

- The code in runic characters of the scholar Saknussemm, that shows an entry to the centre of the globe, brings into play the linguistic competencies of Professor Hardwigg and his nephew. The former detects the presence of various blended languages (Latin, Greek, French and even Hebrew), while the letters have been skilfully mixed according to a combination that Harry incidentally discovers. This code, the manuscript, as well as the traces left by the Icelandic scholar in the 16th century prove a communication attempt between the eras (the 16th and 19th century). This communication is difficult but nevertheless possible.

- Jules Verne plays with the stereotypes that are easily attributed to various nations (Germans are ordered and strict, the Icelandic people are simple and savage and Italians are superstitious). This being so, he puts this little world in communication with each other.
- Furthermore, the professor, thanks to his polyglotism, can communicate with all the characters that he meets, even the scholar Saknussemm through the parchment. Harry can speak in Latin with Professor Fridriksson.
- The words of Hans, who does not speak much, are transcribed in the text in Danish. This creates a gap in the understanding of the professor (who freely uses scientific jargon) and that of Harry who does not know this language. The latter is more capable of deciphering geological traces and thus retracing the evolution of the Earth. Phrases in Latin and, at the end of the story, Italian also appear at various points. There are also these two words from Nordic languages that have been added to the English language: fjord and geyser.
- When Harry loses sight of the stream and his companions, the rocky cavity acts as an acoustic path that serves to

guide and thus allows his to re-establish communication with his uncle.

- The narrator's use of the first person favours young Harry's introspection and, therefore, communication with himself (through dreams and logbooks).

FURTHER REFLECTION

SOME QUESTIONS TO THINK ABOUT…

- What do you think makes this story an adventure novel?
- Jules Verne wrote this novel in 1863. Some have seen him as a clairvoyant. What do you think about this?
- The presence of several languages is noticeable in this novel. What effect does this have?
- What does the author do to make his story as realistic as possible?
- Have the film adaptations kept all the characteristics of the novel?
- Why do you think the author uses internal focalisation?
- Jules Verne wrote during the 19th century, the century of great novelists such as Balzac, Zola, Dickens, Tolstoy, Flaubert, Dostoyevsky, Stendhal, etc. What distinguishes him from all these other authors?
- Do you think that the author wrote this novel for educational purposes?

We want to hear from you!
Leave a comment on your online library
and share your favourite books on social media

FURTHER READING

REFERENCE EDITION

- Verne, J. (1872) *A Journey to the Centre of the Earth*. Trans. Unknown. London: Griffith and Farran.

ADAPTATIONS

- *Journey to the Center of the Earth*. [Film] (1959). Henry Levin. Dir. USA: Twentieth Century Fox Film Corporation.
- *The Fabulous Journey to the Center of the Earth*. [Film] (1976). Juan Piquer Simón. Dir. Spain: Almena Films.
- *Journey to the Center of the Earth*. [Film] (2008). Eric Brevig. Dir. USA: New Line Cinema.
- *Journey to the Center of the Earth*. [Comic book] (1978). Text by Roudolph. Artwork by Renato Polese.
- *Journey to the Center of the Earth*. [Comic book] (2009). Text by Patrice Cartier. Artwork by Édouard Riou.

MORE FROM BRIGHTSUMMARIES.COM

- Reading guide – *Around the World in Eighty Days* by Jules Verne
- Reading guide – *Twenty Thousand Leagues Under the Sea* by Jules Verne
- Reading guide – *The Castle of the Carpathians* by Jules Verne

BOOK ANALYSIS

Bright
Summaries.com

More guides to rediscover
your love of literature

www.brightsummaries.com

www.brightsummaries.com

Ebook EAN: 9782806281104

Paperback EAN: 9782806287724

Legal Deposit: D/2016/12603/661

Digital conception by Primento, the digital partner of publishers.

Made in the USA
Coppell, TX
16 July 2022

80069980R00015